by Fred W. Scott

I am proud to have incredible individuals in my life. First and foremost, I am grateful for my immediate family: **my wife, Paulette, and our children, Neil and Whitney.** They have been my rock, supporting me through every challenge, triumph, and success. Their unwavering presence and love have truly blessed me. I am also thankful for the upbringing provided by my parents, who instilled in my siblings—Wendell, Lisa, and Carol—and me the values that have guided us to become the best versions of ourselves. To all my extended family members, you are loved and valued for your years of support.

I also want to express my gratitude for the positive interactions and friendships I have cultivated. From the close-knit community of my hometown in Richmond, Virginia, to the bonds formed with my classmates at John Marshall High School and Hampton University, each connection enriched my life. From my "Home By The Sea," I want to thank Dr. Carolyn Cooper, my college professor from the School of Education, for being a mentor and friend throughout my life. Your advice has added value to my steps in developing a better me. Having talented classmates influenced my characteristics to enrich my journey. To have a talented classmate, Dr. Melinda Boone, for her exceptional mentorship as well as giving her time to edit this book, I am forever grateful.

Throughout my career and professional journey, I sincerely thank every student and their parents for allowing me to teach and facilitate your learning. For every colleague I have worked with, collaborated with and led within Richmond City and Chesterfield County Public Schools, I thank you for your partnership and inspiration. Special shout out to the wonderful mentors in my education career who assisted me in developing my best talents in education. Every experience allowed me to blossom into the person I am today.

To all my fraternity brothers in Alpha Phi Alpha Fraternity, Inc., thank you for the rewarding journey and the opportunity to coach, mentor, and share best practices. I have learned so much from each of you. Thank you to Alphonso Taylor, Larry Townsend, Sean Bates, Darrell Williams, Carlton Jones, Dr. Larry Frazier, Jermaine Netherly, and many others for your partnership and for serving the brotherhood. Additionally, I received inspiration for writing this book from Brothers Rod Powell, Robert Youngblood, and Robert Dortch your guidance was greatly appreciated.

A special thank you to the many I have worked with in the corporate world of PeopleAdmin and PowerSchool. My experiences and professional growth have allowed me to expand my talents beyond my expectations. Collaborating with every person added tremendous value to my technology, corporate, and educational experiences.

Being blessed with lifelong friends has been important to me in life. I can't name them all from high school to the present, but thank you, Lloyd Bradley, John Townes, Johnny McRoy, Diane Cook, Cobenia Jackson, Jovanni Washington, and Ruth Person for being there for me through the years.

I thank God for guiding my thoughts and words to tell my story. He has blessed me with so many opportunities to empower others. Lastly, thank you for reading, believing, and executing the key elements from my first book. Let me know how the exercises and more are assisting you to find your TalentFRED. Your value and impact will change the world.

Special Thanks

Book Cover & Graphics – Ryan Fontanilla, Ammi Santos
Editing – Dr. Melinda Boone, Ruth Person, Paulette Scott
Fred's Professional Photos – Dante Washington

Fred & Paulette Scott (wife)

INTRODUCTION

Have you ever wondered how to tap into your unique talent realistically with distinct methods, ideas, and strategies that you can implement right away? Year after year and decade after decade, I learned how to grow my talent to expand my reach and develop multifarious skills in many capacities, both professionally and personally. I heard people say from childhood to adulthood, "you are so talented." This compliment has always fueled me to do more and learn more to gain new opportunities to cultivate additional talents. As a little boy who grew up in an urban and low-social economic environment, I loved the visual and performing arts. I learned to play the flute at an early age, as well as exploring drawing and crafting abstract pieces. This was an expression of appreciation passed down from my parents who were trained musicians. It became the gateway to exploring my inner self and tapping into many opportunities in the years to come with my professional career. Tapping into your talents is not only about personal satisfaction but also about optimizing your potential, contributing to others, and finding purpose in your endeavors. It's a crucial aspect of personal and professional development.

Learning to appreciate myself as a creative, inspiring, and motivating being has allowed me to continually grow and motivate others. My journey of self-appreciation and personal growth is ongoing. It has been paramount to continue to nurture and develop these qualities and to be open to learning and adapting along the way. Your ability to appreciate yourself as a creative, inspiring, and motivating individual is not only a gift to yourself but also to those fortunate enough to be part of your life.

In the tapestry of existence, we are all woven with threads of uniqueness, each possessing a distinctive blend of talents, dreams, and aspirations. This book explores the realm of self-discovery and appreciation, a journey into the heart of your inspiration, reflection, and skill.

My professional journey found its roots in the role of a teacher. As a torchbearer of knowledge, I was granted the privilege to guide and nurture young minds, each a unique vessel of potential. My canvas was the realm of mathematics, a subject that not only challenges the intellect but also lays the foundation for critical thinking and problem-solving. As the pages turned in the book of my teaching career, a new chapter unfolded with the advent of technology in education. Computers, the internet, and an array of digital tools stepped onto the classroom stage, transforming the learning landscape.

In my teaching journey, the fusion of mathematics and technology created a unique symphony that fueled my passion for programming and web development with graphic design. I wanted my once-static classroom to be transformed into a dynamic canvas where algorithms danced with numbers and students found the joy of developing skills and eventually a talent for mathematics. Yet, beyond the code, my mission became personal— motivating students, promoting joy within the subject, and inspiring them to join this vibrant blend of knowledge and creativity. My heart was definitively to cultivate my teaching methodologies and student learning.

My journey reflects a deep commitment to education, technology, and community empowerment. By obtaining a master's degree from Columbia University in Instructional Technology, I equipped myself with the knowledge and skills to effectively integrate instruction and technology in innovative ways while leading others to find their talent with technology.

My unwavering dedication to enhancing opportunities in both the classroom and the community is a testament to my commitment to developing my talent and others. Whether in fraternity leadership or various roles, I've strived to make a positive impact. Beyond the titles of teacher, tech leader, principal, professional developer, performance manager, education consultant, and solution engineer, my true mission in life is clear: to passionately empower others to uncover their talents and potential. This drive defines my journey and underscores a deeply ingrained commitment to uplifting those around me as well as new people I encounter.

TalentFRED is my way of helping people discover their value and make a meaningful impact. I share my experiences and knowledge to inspire and motivate others to pursue their goals, understand their talent, and find fulfillment in their personal and professional learning journeys.

So how did I get the nickname *TalentFRED*? In my last role in K-12, I directed my district in performance evaluation and supervision using a product called TalentED (*formerly by PeopleAdmin now PowerSchool*), and one principal in a meeting amongst his peers said, Fred, you are now TalentFRED because I see your passion for learning, technology, support, authenticity, and clear use of visuals. Through my K–12 years, I developed extraordinary talents beyond my expectations. Thus, the name was attached to me from that point and into the corporate EdTech world.

TalentFRED transcends beyond me; it is me saying to you that everyone has the power to triumph, achieve, lead, educate, nurture, and thrive to be the best YOU.

Let's explore TalentFRED!

- ❖ **T = Triumphing You**
- ❖ **A = Achieving Your Best**
- ❖ **L = Leading You & Others**
- ❖ **E = Educating You**
- ❖ **N = Nurturing You**
- ❖ **T = Thriving Beyond You**

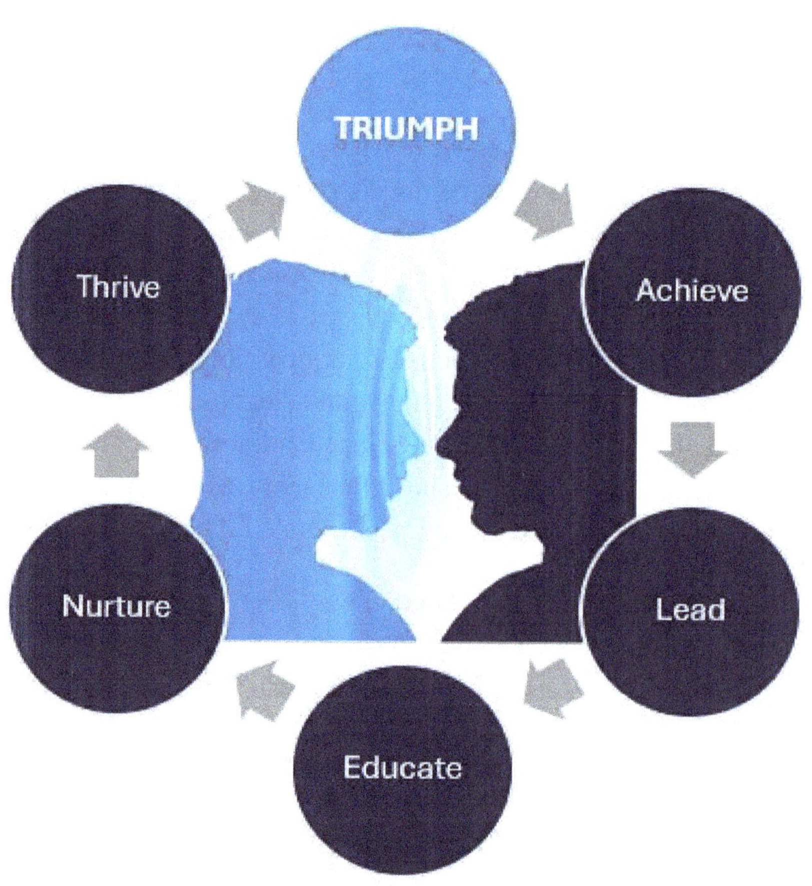
TRIUMPH
Thrive
Achieve
Nurture
Lead
Educate

Over the journey of my life, wandering through various channels of interests, activities, and discoveries, I have always known when I participated in any activity, organization, and more if it tapped into the inner core of feeling self-worth, value, and impact. I wanted to know more, learn more, and be more inside that space. Embracing this awareness can guide you in making choices that align with your values and passions. It can also inspire you to seek out opportunities for growth and impact in areas that resonate with your innermost desires.

Instead of viewing obstacles or setbacks as weaknesses or challenges, I see them as opportunities for learning, development, and growth. This perspective enables you to approach new opportunities with enthusiasm and confidence, knowing that you can overcome any obstacles that may arise along the way.

Starting with the concept of "Triumph" sets a powerful tone for your journey of self-discovery and talent development. By beginning with a mindset of success and victory, you're setting yourself up for a positive and empowering experience.

Here's why starting with "T" meaning Triumph is significant:

- **Positive mindset:** By focusing on triumph, you're cultivating a positive mindset that emphasizes your ability to overcome obstacles and achieve success. Think about it: having this mindset can help you approach challenges with confidence and resilience.

I have approached a significant part of my life with a positive mindset that I can win in the end. A positive mindset has power! Practice using this power to focus on your worth and value. Remember, your TALENT will make an IMPACT.

- **Empower**: Starting with triumph empowers you to take control of your narrative and shape your pathway. It encourages you to believe in your potential and take proactive steps toward realizing your goals and aspirations. The development of your talent will empower you to investigate, discover, and learn.

- **Motivation:** The idea of triumph can serve as a powerful source of inspiration, inspiring you to pursue your passions, explore new opportunities, and push past your comfort zone. Nothing motivates me more than being in the zone of being happy about my skill set, value, and impact. I learned that it motivates the opportunities and future pathways or skills sitting to the left and right of your visual acuity.

- **Discover ME:** Triumphing in the journey of finding your best skills and talents signifies a process of uncovering your strengths, passions, and God-given abilities. To discover me, I had to embrace me and my potential to uncover possibilities as well as embrace impossibilities. Nothing feels better to me than discovering that I can do something that I thought was impossible. I learned over the years that you make possibilities out of things that are impossible.

Concept	Identify Time in Your Life	What were the results?
A. Learning from **failure**		
B. Identifying when you were **resilient**		
C. Being **flexible or adaptable**		
D. Recognizing when you **grew or improved** from a skill, activity, or opportunity		
Formulate a sentence to fill in the blanks:		

I learned that when I fail at an opportunity, I

______________________________________.

It taught me I am resilient because

______________________________________.

Developing the ability to adapt and be flexible assists me to understand that I

______________________________________.

So I have grown with my skills, talents, or opportunities by the
following____

____

____

____

Engaging in this activity provides an opportunity for you to reflect on various aspects of life, including experiences of failure, resilience, flexibility, and personal growth.

Remember to embrace failure. To triumph, you must discover your talent, one must learn to fail. If humans did everything right every time, we would be robots, or even worse, the Stepford Wives. I learned that each time I failed at a skill, activity, or task, I learned how to be flexible. This flexibility was difficult for me because I thought, … me? However, you fall and get up again, and a new day begins. Adapt, adapt, and adapt more to overcome obstacles, which will make you stronger. Looking back on each of these opportunities, it kept me agile, and I adopted a growth mindset. By embracing failure, cultivating flexibility, and resilience, and adopting a growth mindset, you've embarked on a journey of self-discovery and personal growth that will undoubtedly lead to the realization of your talents and aspirations. Your willingness to learn from failure and adapt to new challenges sets you apart as someone who is not afraid to pursue their passions and overcome obstacles along the way. Keep embracing the journey and remember that each failure is a stepping stone toward your ultimate triumph.

Starting at the beginning of finding yourself can be seen as your greatest opportunity.

Triumphing you means to find your talent. This suggests the idea of overcoming obstacles or limitations to discover and nurture your innate abilities or skills. It implies a journey of self-discovery and personal growth, where one triumphs over doubts, fears, or external challenges to uncover and develop one's talents.

Let's do another **Activity (1B)** on how you approach this process using the chart to focus on the **6 six concepts**, meanings, and your reflections.

Now, complete the table below with your responses:

Concept	Meaning	Your Reflection
Self-Reflection	Take time to reflect on your interests, passions, and experiences. Think about activities that you enjoy and excel in, as well as areas where you feel a sense of fulfillment.	
Exploration	Be open to trying new things and exploring different areas of interest. Experiment with various activities, hobbies, or fields to see what resonates.	

Feedback	Seek feedback from others, such as friends, family, teachers, or mentors, about your strengths and areas for improvement. Their perspectives can offer valuable insights into your talents and potential areas of focus.	
Practice and Perseverance	Once you've identified your talents or interests, dedicate time and effort to develop and refine them. Practice regularly, set goals, and persist through challenges or setbacks.	

Continuous Learning	Keep learning and expanding your skills and knowledge in your chosen area of talent. Stay curious, seek out growth opportunities, and remain open to feedback and new experiences.	
Believe in Yourself	Cultivate self-confidence and belief in your abilities. Trust in your capacity to succeed and overcome obstacles along the way.	

By triumphing over obstacles and embracing your journey of self-discovery, you can uncover your talents and realize your full potential. After going through Activity 1B, ask yourself these guiding questions:

- In your self-reflection, what do you feel are skills, attributes, etc. are specific talents you wish to explore more?

  ____.

- After identifying what hobbies, activities, or interests may be in your wheelhouse, what would you consider your top 3 things?
  (1) _________ (2) __________ (3) __________.
- Hearing feedback from friends, family, or professional colleagues, what do they say are the skills or attributes you have as gift(s)?

  ______________________________________ .

- Based on your responses above, what steps would you like to pursue to ensure you are developing your talent and skills to their optimum?

  ____

  ____

  _____________________________________ .

As I embarked on the journey of marrying my joy with my professional aspirations, the lyrics of Anita Baker's *"You Bring Me Joy"* echoed in my mind. In 1986, amidst the excitement of getting married, I yearned to discover the same level of fulfillment in my career. The key takeaway from the song, *"When I lose my way, your love*

comes smiling on me," struck a chord deep within me. I realized that my passion for teaching, learning, and technology held the potential to propel me toward a future brimming with opportunities. I wanted that same love to shine in my profession.

With this realization fueling my ambition, I committed myself to furthering my understanding of teaching mathematics. Returning to school to delve deeper into my field, I eagerly absorbed knowledge and honed my skills. Engaging in professional development workshops on instructional strategies empowered me to refine my approach to teaching, particularly in terms of fostering student engagement. Each endeavor, whether in the classroom or through workshops, contributed to perfecting my craft and amplifying my passion for education.

I discovered that my love for teaching and learning extended beyond the confines of traditional academia. Embracing every facet of the educational experience, I found joy in creativity, organization, data analysis, mathematics, technology, and the visual arts. Each element intertwined seamlessly, enriching my professional journey and reaffirming my commitment to continuous growth.

As I poured myself into the art of teaching and learning, I embraced both current practices and emerging trends in education. This relentless pursuit of knowledge and skill development became the cornerstone of my personal and professional triumphs. I accepted that overcoming obstacles and seizing opportunities were inherent to my journey of self-discovery and advancement.

These meaningful activities weren't just about professional growth for me; they became a journey to find joy in my talents. By wholeheartedly pursuing excellence and embracing every chance to grow, I overcame challenges and carved out a career that aligns with my values, passion, and purpose.

For me, the journey to **triumph** began by uncovering joy in my talents. It's been a personal exploration, driven by my passion and unwavering commitment. Each obstacle I faced became an opportunity, and every experience contributed to my growth, both personally and professionally. In this chapter, you have just received a heartfelt invitation to continue to join me to support your journey, where the key is to discover joy in your unique talents and triumph over every challenge that comes your way. Whether you're a student, young professional, or someone with seasoned professional experience, you've just uncovered the tools to **triumph you** in the discovery of your talent(s).

Triumph
Thrive
ACHIEVE
Nurture
Lead
Educate

It's common for the concept of being "*the best*" to feel intimidated or overwhelmed, especially during adolescence, when there'soften pressure to excel in various areas of life. However, as you've discovered, the notion of "doing your best" is much more empowering and attainable.

Approaching skill development with a focus on personal progress is likc trying *to fold a fitted sheet, which I struggle to get right. It might seem tricky, but it's a game-changer.* Shifting away from constant comparison with others to the unique journey of mastering your talents brings a sense of humor to the often-frustrating process. Recognizing that your path is as distinct as wrestling with a fitted sheet. Progress outshines perfection and becomes the comedy script for greater self-compassion and resilience.

I want you in this chapter to focus on refining your skills, which cultivates a positive mindset and promotes continuous improvement and personal satisfaction. It's all about pursuing excellence on your terms, setting meaningful goals, and enjoying the learning process along the way.

As you continue to pursue your passions and aspirations, remember that your best is always evolving. *What may be your best today might look different tomorrow, and that's okay.* I suggest that you don't beat yourself like I do sometimes in the process. The key is to remain committed to your growth, embrace challenges as opportunities for learning, and celebrate your progress, no matter how small. In doing so, you'll unlock your true potential and find fulfillment in the journey of self-discovery and personal development.

Like everyone else, I've faced failure even when I gave my best. It can be tough, especially with the pressures of today's global and social expectations. Yet, your ability to bounce back and learn from these moments is truly impressive. I've learned to see each new day as a chance for a fresh start.

The idea that "*the next day is a new day*" reflects a growth mindset, which is essential for personal development and success. It's about recognizing that setbacks are growth opportunities, and that each failure brings valuable lessons that can inform future endeavors.

The analogy of "*saving the best for last*," as expressed in Vanessa Williams' song, resonates with the notion of strategically showcasing your skills and talents. It's about timing and presentation—ensuring that when you can demonstrate your abilities to others, you do so with confidence and excellence. By reflecting on past experiences, investigating different approaches, and adapting your strategies, you can continually refine your skills and increase the likelihood of success in future endeavors.

In the end, it's your resilience, adaptability, and dedication to getting better that push you forward toward reaching your full potential. Facing both challenges and triumphs, you gain a deeper understanding of yourself, paving the way for growth and success in all areas of life.

In this chapter, let's explore why it will be important to **achieve your best** by developing effective goals, consistent habits, effective strategies, and assessing your performance. When you are exploring skills and talents, each one of those areas of goals, habits, strategies, and assessment plays into achieving your best over time.

Setting effective goals, cultivating consistent habits, developing strategies, and regularly assessing performance are all crucial components of achieving one's best potential.

- **Your Effective Goals:** Goals provide direction and motivation. Clear goals assist you in clarifying what you want to achieve and provide a roadmap for getting there. There are many examples of formulating SMART goals. SMART stands for specific, measurable, achievable, relevant, and time bound. By setting effective goals, you can laser-focus on your efforts and track your progress according to your plan.

- **Your Consistent Habits:** Habits are the building blocks of success. By establishing positive habits, you create a framework for consistent action that moves you closer to your goals. Whether it's practicing a skill daily, exercising regularly, or dedicating time to study, consistent habits help reinforce progress over time. A great book to delve into is "Atomic Habits" by James Clear.

- **Your Effective Strategies:** Strategies are the plans or approaches you use to achieve your goals. They involve identifying the most efficient and effective ways to reach your objectives. This might involve breaking down large goals into smaller, manageable tasks, leveraging resources, seeking guidance from mentors, or experimenting with different approaches until you find what works best for you.

- **Your Performance:** Regularly assessing your performance allows you to gauge progress, identify areas for improvement, and make necessary adjustments to your goals, habits, and strategies. This could involve tracking metrics, seeking feedback from others, reflecting on your experiences, and being open to learning from both successes and failures.

In your journey of discovering your unique talents, I suggest you start incorporating these elements and building a personalized framework for growth. Each part supports the others, working together to help you gradually realize your full potential. Staying adaptable and open-minded in this process ensures continuous improvement; always aim for your best self.

Let's dive into some exercises to develop talents using goals, habits, strategies, and performance assessment:

Goal Setting Exercise:

- Start by identifying a talent or skill you want to develop.
- Set a specific, measurable goal related to this talent.
- Break down your goal into smaller, actionable steps.

- *Vision Board*: Write down your goal and the steps needed to achieve it and keep them somewhere visible as a reminder of your commitment.

Identify one talent or skill you want to develop.

____

1. Your GOAL:

____

2. Your ACTION STEPS:

____

____

____

3. Your RESULTS:

____

____

4. Your REFLECTIONS:

____

____

Building Your Habits Exercise:

- Identify habits that will support your goal.
- Start small and gradually increase the intensity or duration of your habits over time. Consistency is key, so aim to practice your chosen habit every day.
- Use habit-tracking tools or apps to monitor your progress and hold yourself accountable. Here are some apps:
  - **Streaks** *(iOS, Apple Watch, macOS)*
  - **Habitify** *(iOS, Android, macOS, Web)*
  - **Habitica** *(iOS, Android, Web)*

Experiment with different strategies to make your habits stick, such as pairing them with existing routines or rewarding yourself for consistency.

Here are two Habit Formation graphic organizers to build your talent.

Habit Formation Loop adapted from
(The Behavioral Science Behind Pillsy | by Jeff LeBrun |
Medium (LeBrun, 2017)

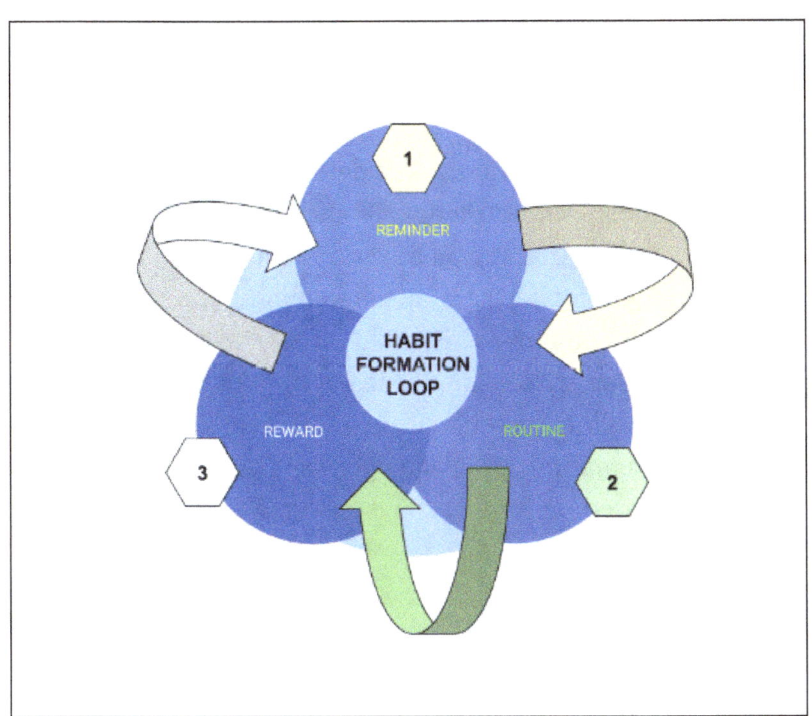

1	Celebrate & Maintain Habits
2	Reflect on Your Progress
3	Reward Yourself
4	Share Your Success
5	Continuously Learn and Grow
6	Create a Case Study
7	Tips for Maintaining Successful Habits

Strategic Planning Exercise:

- Evaluate different strategies for achieving your goal. Research instructional materials, seek advice from experts, and explore various learning techniques.
- Develop a plan of action outlining the strategies you will employ. This could include scheduling practice sessions, seeking feedback from mentors or peers, and incorporating diverse learning methods.
- Remain flexible and open to adjusting your strategies based on feedback and evolving circumstances.

Regularly review and refine your plan to ensure it remains aligned with your goals and conducive to your learning progress.

Notes: ____

____

____

____

____

____

____

____

Create Your Personal Strategic Plan by Carol Vernon (Vernon, n.d.) provides effective steps on personal development planning.

These steps provide a structured approach to setting and achieving your goals. **Use the checklist below:**

☐ Find time: Allocate dedicated time in your schedule to focus on developing your personal strategic plan.

☐ Clarify your values: Reflect on your core values, beliefs, and principles that guide your decisions and actions.

☐ Create your mission statement: Develop a clear and concise statement that articulates your purpose, what you aim to achieve, and how you intend to make a positive impact.

☐ Do a SWOT analysis on yourself: Conduct a SWOT (Strengths, Weaknesses, Opportunities, Threats) analysis to assess your internal strengths and weaknesses.

☐ Create your goals: Set specific, measurable, achievable, relevant, and time-bound (SMART) goals based on your mission statement and SWOT analysis.

☐ Determine what support you need to stay accountable to your plan: Identify resources, mentors, accountability partners, or support networks that can help you stay focused and committed to achieving your goals. I cannot stress how important this will be in your plan. Having a support system can provide encouragement, feedback, and accountability throughout your journey.

Performance Assessment Exercise:

- Set benchmarks or milestones to track your performance over time. These could be weekly progress check-ins or periodic assessments of specific skills.
- Solicit feedback from others, such as teachers, mentors, or peers, to gain different perspectives on your progress and areas for improvement.
- Reflect on your performance regularly. Identify strengths and weaknesses, celebrate successes, and brainstorm strategies for addressing challenges.
- Adjust your goals, habits, and strategies as needed based on your performance assessments, maintaining a proactive approach to your talent development journey.

Notes: _______________________________________

____

____

____

____

Assess your strengths and weaknesses:
____

Reflect on your goal(s) and strategies:
____

Identify steps or strategies you would repeat:
____

Review the opportunities and resources and their impact: _______________________________

List other factors that impacted your success or failure: _______________________________

By following these tips and incorporating them into your personal development plan, you can effectively assess your progress, set meaningful goals, and continue to evolve and improve over time.

Think of these exercises as the GPS for your talent journey - they provide a clear roadmap for growth and progress, minus the robotic voice from Waze or Google Maps telling you to turn left at 500 feet. It's like a treasure hunt where consistent practice, smart planning, and occasionally checking your map (or maybe your phone) help you uncover the hidden gems of your potential. So, grab your compass (or smartphone) and let the talent adventure begin!

I have highlighted some crucial points about the journey of your talent development. It's important to recognize that achieving one's best and growing talent is indeed not an easy feat—it requires dedication, hard work, and tenacity. Consistency, practice, and authentic reflection are essential components of this process.

Finding your joy and satisfaction in the pursuit of talent development is key. While the journey may have its challenges, the progress and growth achieved along the way will be rewarding.

When you incorporate these principles into your talent development, it's like having that same GPS that helps you navigate challenges, seize opportunities, and ultimately reach your full potential. Just like any journey, it requires patience, resilience, and a commitment to continuous improvement.

For me, striving for excellence and honing my talent means repeating the process, and shaping my reputation both professionally and personally. Regular practice not only improves my expertise but also contributes to building a solid standing in my chosen field. Following these suggested activities is my way of coaching you to identify your unique pathway of skills.

Repeating things builds trustworthiness, and reliability, crucial qualities in any job. Consistently delivering top-notch work and showcasing your skills make you a trusted and respected figure in your field. You need to prove that your style is your "ikigai." I love this concept. Let's find the significance of i-ki-gai!!!

Understanding your "*ikigai* (*Ikigai: The Japanese Secret to a Joyful Life*, 2022)," a Japanese concept that translates to "reason for being" or "the reason for getting up in the morning," is a powerful tool for personal growth and fulfillment. Your ikigai lies at the intersection of what you love, what you are good at, what the world needs, and what you can be paid for. By identifying activities or pursuits that fulfill each of these criteria, you can uncover your true purpose and direction in life.

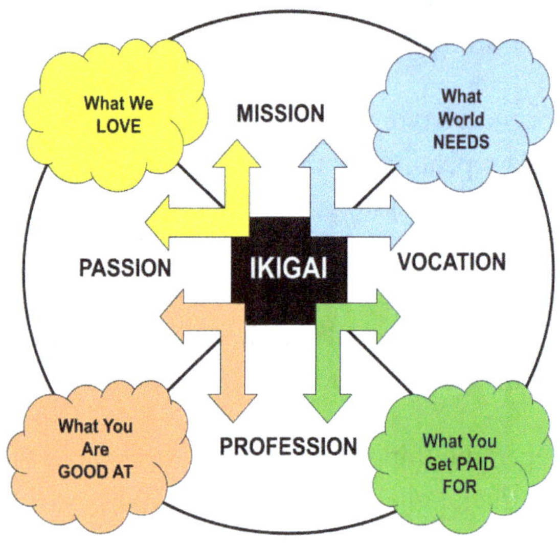

To cultivate **TalentFRED**, I've always turned inward, reflecting on my passions, values, strengths, and dreams. This has been crucial in shaping my talents. As you embark on this journey of achieving you, connecting with your inner self and fostering self-awareness will bring you clarity about what truly brings you joy and meaning.

I encourage you to incorporate these principles into your life. By doing so, you can continue nurturing your passion, honing your skills, and pursuing a path that aligns with your ikigai. This journey of self-discovery and personal growth won't just bring greater fulfillment but will also empower you to make meaningful contributions to the world around you. *Achieving you is like sharpening your knife, but don't forget about polishing the fork and spoon.*

Notes:

____
____
____
____
____
____
____
____
____
____
____
____
____
____

"Reflection time is important for YOU."

Triumph
Thrive
Achieve
Nurture
LEAD
Educate

In this chapter, we will delve into two essential areas of developing your talent: **yourself and others**. Throughout my journey, I discovered that my triumphs and achievements served as the catalyst to ignite my inner drive and enhance my skills, shaping my unique talents. From a young age, I harbored a deep desire to become an educator, dedicated to helping children discover strategies to unlock their fullest potential. However, it took me years to uncover how to effectively leverage my innate gift to enrich the classroom experience for all students. One thing remained clear: *serving as a facilitator of learning compelled me to explore how I could harness my talents to lead myself effectively, while also guiding others towards realizing their maximum potential.*

Embrace the notion of leadership when it comes to **yourself**. I realized in high school, I needed to investigate learning and leading me. It was a struggle to mentally understand until later in life, but I instinctively knew that I needed to venture down this road to elevate my talent. When taking charge of your path, it's crucial to ask: *What steps can I take towards mastering the process of unleashing my talent?*

Now that you have navigated through previous chapters with a toolbox of skills, it's time to unveil the leader in you. My suggestion to you is to be the force that seizes opportunities. I want you to lead your self-leadership pathway with command while showcasing your talents. You need to adopt this philosophy, "*I will make a lasting impact wherever I go.*" This is your time to shine.

Self-leadership, as defined by research, refers to the process by which individuals take personal responsibility for guiding and directing themselves toward achieving their goals and objectives. You unveil yourself; this means involving self-awareness, self-regulation, and self-motivation to effectively manage your thoughts, emotions, and behaviors in pursuit of your desired outcomes.

In my life's journey, I discovered that doing research is essential. The research on self-leadership focuses on strategies and techniques individuals can employ to enhance their performance and effectiveness. These strategies may include setting goals, managing time and resources efficiently, maintaining a positive mindset, seeking feedback, and continuously learning and adapting to new challenges. Well, this has been the root cause of my development regarding leading myself.

Self-leadership is pivotal for effective leadership. Those with stalwart self-leadership skills inspire and influence others, handle complexity well, and succeed in personal and professional aspects. My interest in leadership is driven by a desire to empower others.

I am sure you may be asking yourself, "*Will this be important to me?*" Studies have also shown that self-leadership can lead to increased job satisfaction, higher levels of motivation, and improved performance outcomes.

Discovering the leader within starts with you:

- ❖ **Look Within:** Take a moment to understand your strengths, weaknesses, values, and goals.
- ❖ **Inspiration Around:** Find inspiration in leaders you admire, learning from their journey.
- ❖ **Skill Boost:** Work on improving how you communicate, make decisions, and understand emotions.
- ❖ **Step Up:** Don't shy away from opportunities; showcase your unique abilities when they arise.
- ❖ **Own Your Impact:** Reflect on your actions and consider how they affect those around you.
- ❖ **Growth Amid Challenges:** Embrace challenges; they are chances for personal and professional growth.
- ❖ **Build Connections:** Cultivate strong relationships for collaborative success.
- ❖ **Stay Flexible:** Regularly assess your progress and adapt your strategies as needed. This journey is yours—embrace it.

You may or may not be thinking, that he wants me to navigate the path of self-leadership independently. I am saying that we need to break it down together. Take the suggestions above, in no particular order, and start reviewing up to *four elements* you wish to enrich. **Remember, the best rewards often come from getting comfortable with the uncomfortable.** You are empowered to broaden your perspective, commit to continuous learning, and, frankly, just take one step at a time. You can cultivate your self-leadership skills, unlocking your full potential on this talent journey.

Getting to know yourself is key, especially if you're aiming to lead. Before guiding others, you've got to nail self-leadership, which has **four pillars:** *figuring yourself out, being cool with who you are, handling yourself, and always growing.* These pillars set the stage for good leadership by encouraging you to be real, stay strong, and keep getting better.

There were short-and long-term discoveries in mastering my distinct talents. **TalentFRED** suggests to you, to be who you are and not imitate but appreciate. Then you become cool with who you are as a human being to implement the skills to master your talent(s).

"Self-leadership is having a developed sense of who you are, what you can do, where you are going coupled with the ability to influence your communication, emotions, and behavior on the way to getting there." (Bryant, Kazan 2012)

Let's explore Activity 3A - Adapted from (*Self-Leadership as a Prerequisite for Success*, 2023)

Guiding Questions to Complete:

1. What are my self-awareness attributes?

   ____

   ____

   ____

2. What behaviors do I exemplify when regulating my processes?

   ____

   ____

   ____

3. How do I motivate myself to stay on track with goals, strategies, and more?

   ____

   ____

____

____

____

Leading oneself serves as the bedrock for expressing all your other attributes, including knowledge, skills, abilities, passions, and values. It echoes the sentiment of Michael Jackson's song "*Man in the Mirror*," emphasizing the importance of self-reflection and personal transformation. Just as the song suggests, initiating change begins with oneself, paving the way for self-satisfaction and growth.

If you have aspirations of leading others, let's discuss leadership beyond you. Leadership extends beyond oneself and encompasses various aspects that involve guiding and inspiring others toward a common goal.

Here are some key elements of leadership beyond the individual and my experiences (★FRED) under each element:

Vision: Leaders inspire and motivate by articulating a compelling vision! You want to formulate a clear picture of the future to build and unite others around that shared goal.

- ★ *FRED: As a central-level leader for Instructional Technology, I was entrusted with the responsibility of crafting a vision and strategy for integrating technology seamlessly into educational practices. I organized a team of new employees with expertise in various content areas and grade levels. This team was tasked with inspiring, coaching, training, and supporting educators in effectively utilizing technology to enhance student learning and teacher pedagogy. By aligning team members based on content and level, we ensured educators received tailored support and guidance from experts, facilitating the successful integration of technology across classrooms and productivity practices.*

Communication: **Leaders communicate clearly! They should be good at talking and active listening, encouraging open conversations to make sure everyone is on the same page.**

★ *FRED: In my previous roles as a teacher leader and school principal, I prioritized aligning with the school district's vision, goals, and improvement benchmarks for student success. This involved formulating clear messages and communicating school opportunities to all stakeholders, supported by data analysis targeting areas for growth, addressing gaps, and celebrating achievements. By fostering professional learning communities, both as a teacher leader and principal, I honed my skills in effective oral and written communication, active listening, and collaboration, enabling me to engage with diverse stakeholders and facilitate meaningful dialogue to drive positive change within the school community.*

 Leaders empower others! It's about giving them the authority and resources they need, trusting in their abilities, and supporting their growth.

★ *FRED: As a past President of my fraternity at the state level, I focused on empowering each chapter president to lead effectively. This involved empowering them to implement programs, communicate changes, and provide the necessary tools to support their work within their chapters. I trusted in their abilities to execute their roles and responsibilities. Additionally, I learned the importance of inspecting their work, encouraging them to reflect on their findings, and respecting them as leaders. This approach fostered a culture of accountability, collaboration, and mutual respect, ultimately contributing to the success and cohesion of the fraternity at the state level.*

Decision-Making: **Leaders are responsible for making timely and well-informed decisions! They weigh various perspectives, gather relevant information, and consider the potential impact of their decisions on stakeholders.**

★ *FRED: As a central-level leader (Professional Development/HR Specialist) overseeing performance evaluation for the entire school district, I spearheaded the formation of a think tank team. This team was tasked with assessing and synthesizing our evaluation processes, technology tool strategies, and best practices. By gathering diverse perspectives, we aimed to provide valuable insights to guide school administrators in their work and its impact on instruction. Through collaborative efforts and critical analysis, we sought to enhance the effectiveness and efficiency of our evaluation methods, ultimately contributing to improved educational outcomes district-wide.*

Inspiration: Leaders lead by example! They inspire others through their actions, attitudes, and behaviors, fostering a sense of purpose and commitment among team members.

★ *FRED: As the Mathematics Department Chair, I embraced the challenge of analyzing student performance on district or school-wide assessments to identify areas for improvement. I saw myself as an inspirer and multiplier, leading by example to model effective actions, boost morale, and foster a culture of collegial sharing and learning. By aligning our efforts with the overarching goal of student achievement, I encouraged my team to commit to a pursuit of excellence. Together, we worked collaboratively to implement strategies, engage in professional learning, and continuously seek growth opportunities, ensuring that our efforts were always directed towards enhancing student outcomes.*

Collaboration: Leaders know that collaboration is essential for achieving shared goals and leveraging the

collective expertise of others. Leaders foster a culture where diverse perspectives are valued, and individuals work together towards common objectives.

★ *FRED: In my role as a Senior Business Education Consultant with an EdTech company, my team and I focused on optimizing our approach to managing our book of business, enhancing customer engagement, and streamlining client documentation. We collaborated to find ways to work smarter, not harder, by identifying efficiencies and leveraging technology where possible. Our goal was to enrich our team's processes and culture while fostering different perspectives. Through effective collaboration and continuous improvement, we aimed to deliver exceptional service to our clients and achieve success as a cohesive team.*

Accountability: **Leaders hold themselves and others accountable! They establish clear expectations, provide feedback, and ensure that individuals take ownership of their responsibilities.**

★ *FRED: As an Instructional Technology Director in my district, I worked with a large team that included team leaders. Together, we developed expectations for professional growth goals, established measurable benchmarks for observations, and implemented a documentation system in our database tool. We set clear guidelines for team leaders to support their teams effectively, ensuring that evaluation metrics reflected ownership of their work. This approach empowered team leaders to provide guidance and mentorship while fostering accountability and growth within our team. This was also applicable when I was a school principal.*

Adaptability: Leaders must be adaptable and responsive to new opportunities! They embrace change, encourage innovation, and help others navigate uncertainty with resilience and agility.

★ *FRED: During my tenure as the President/District Director of my fraternity in Virginia, the onset of the pandemic necessitated a significant shift in our operational approach. Recognizing the importance of maintaining brotherhood engagement despite the challenges, we swiftly adapted our processes, programs, and membership strategies to the digital landscape. It became evident that leveraging various technology tools would be crucial in facilitating ongoing engagement and support for our members.*

To address this, we focused on understanding and accommodating adult learning styles in the virtual environment. We explored a range of digital tools and platforms to identify the most effective ones for our fraternity's needs. This involved assessing factors such as accessibility, usability, and functionality to ensure seamless integration into our operations. Through strategic planning and collaboration, we successfully navigated the transition to virtual engagement, fostering a sense of connection and continuity within our fraternity despite the physical distance imposed by the pandemic. Our commitment to embracing technology as a means of maintaining brotherhood engagement underscored our resilience and adaptability in the face of unprecedented challenges.

Ethical Leadership: Leaders are morally and socially responsible! Leaders prioritize integrity, honesty, and fairness, serving as role models for ethical behavior.

★ *FRED: As the School Improvement Manager at my middle school, our team faced critical discussions regarding teachers' attendance, professionalism, and communication with parents. Addressing these areas, we collaboratively developed strategies and actions to enhance the school handbook, implement professional growth workshops, and provide examples of effective parent communication.*

Together, we brainstormed various approaches and activities, committing to serve as facilitators and role models for our peers. Over several months, we diligently implemented these initiatives. As a result, administrators observed significant improvements across all targeted areas, including instructional delivery. Our collective efforts and commitment to continuous improvement made a positive impact on the school community.

Servant Leadership: **Leaders prioritize the needs of others over their own! They focus on serving and supporting others. It is essential to foster a culture of empathy, compassion, and servant-heartedness, striving to make a positive difference in the lives of those they lead.**

★ *FRED: As Chapter President of my fraternity, we initiated a partnership with the Big Brothers Big Sisters program to mentor elementary boys. A dedicated group of men aimed to provide social and academic support to these young men. I invited the school principal to a chapter meeting to discuss the dynamics of her male students, particularly the need for positive role models.*

Collectively, we decided to fulfill our fraternity's special project and education program by mentoring these young men and supporting the school with other activities. The feedback from both our brothers and the school was overwhelmingly positive and uplifting, reflecting the meaningful impact of our collaboration and commitment to community service.

In my leadership journey, expanding as well as stretching my horizons has not only allowed me to feature my skills in leadership but also to mentor and coach others, as well as nurturing future leaders. I've served as a coach and mentor in education, community, and my fraternity, honing my ability to guide others to triumph and achievement, empowering them to reach their full potential.

Before leading anyone, start by leading yourself. It sets the foundation for leading others, a chance to empower and uplift those around you. What's your take on self-leadership in your journey? *Write a sentence or two from your perspective.*

____

____

____

____

____

*~

Leadership beyond you is about inspiring, empowering, and enabling others to reach their full potential and achieve collective success. It requires a combination of vision, communication, empowerment, collaboration, and ethical conduct to lead and influence others toward shared goals effectively.

"Leading Others" is another focal point of this chapter, tailored for you as aspiring leaders in your talent journey. My intent here is to share my varied experiences. I'll share my insights to coach you as an aspiring leader. Regardless of your current role or position in life, my goal is to encourage you to explore leadership opportunities and make a meaningful impact through your talent. Let's dive in and explore the journey of leadership together!

Leading others involves sharing and teaching them how to uncover and implement your success strategies. Teaching is not only a way to ensure personal success but also uplifts those you lead. That uplift is a feeling that's indescribable and elevates your talent. However, it's crucial to understand your leadership style before embarking on your journey. If you are already on the journey, use the information to affirm or collaborate. Knowing your style helps you effectively communicate your vision and goals, fostering a positive environment for yourself and your team. I love the opportunity to mentor young people and adults to discover their distinct gifts or talents, I've gained reassurance in my steps, processes, and the utilization of TalentFRED.

To lead others, I want to walk you through learning the various styles of leadership that are crucial for comprehending oneself and achieving success in any journey, whether it's in education, business, law, medicine, or any other field. Understanding and being able to draw upon different leadership styles as needed is essential for navigating diverse situations effectively.

When delving into the study of different leadership styles, you can be overwhelmed as you encounter a vast array of information and research, offering valuable insights into effective leadership practices.

Let's discuss LEADERSHIP STYLES—it's like perusing flavors in an ice cream shop! Some flavors will suit you, and some will not. You just need to be aware of them all.

· **Autocratic leaders** are the solo decision-makers, laying down the law and keeping things in check. This style is the *do-as-I say style!*

· **Democratic leaders** are the team players, getting everyone's input before making the final call. This style is *having the desire to have all the ingredients in one ice cream cone!*

· Now, if you're into the hands-off approach—*I called this the untouchables or don't bother*, **Laissez-faire leader** is your go-to. This style has minimal interference and maximum team freedom.

· **Transactional leaders** are all about give and take. *I call this style the push/pull effect, or I like it one day and not the other.* Clear expectations, rewards for hitting the mark, and a little friendly penalty for those who miss it.

· **Transformational leaders,** *I call this style the person who thinks big dreams, inspiration, and motivational boosting.* They're all about creating a great vibe, elevating innovation, and fostering growth in the team. The taste always has a boost of flavor.

· **Servant leaders** are the ultimate team supporters. Putting their team's needs first, leading by example, and being the champion of encouragement. *I call this style of thinking about others first all the time.*

· **Charismatic leaders** are the superstars or standouts of leadership. *I call this style the person with a boatload of charisma, vision, and passion, who can turn a group of people into a motivated group to accomplish almost anything.*

· **Authentic leaders**, *I call this style the real deal. The flavor is always consistent with value and impact.* Leading with honesty and integrity, they're on a mission to build people's trust and credibility, leading one step at a time with purpose and strategy. This one is a favorite of mine.

Phew, that's the leadership lineup of flavors! When you see them, all displayed and acted upon by others, ask yourself which style suits your taste.

> Leadership is like making an *ice cream sundae*. Autocratic leaders decide independently, like classic chocolate. Democratic leaders involve the team, resembling an open toppings bar. Laissez-faire leaders offer creative freedom, akin to soft-serve vanilla. Transactional leaders reward success, similar to adding a cherry to meeting goals. Transformational leaders inspire, while servant leaders prioritize their team. Charismatic leaders bring a captivating flair, and authentic leaders build trust.

I had the opportunity to go to the Center of Situational Leadership to take the various workshops, sessions, and certification programs. Studying and certifying in Situational Leadership® provided me with valuable insights into effective leadership practices. Situational Leadership® emphasizes the importance of adapting leadership styles based on the needs of individual team members and the specific circumstances of a situation. This approach helped me to recognize that there is no one-size-fits-all leadership style and encourages leaders to be flexible and responsive to the changing dynamics within people.

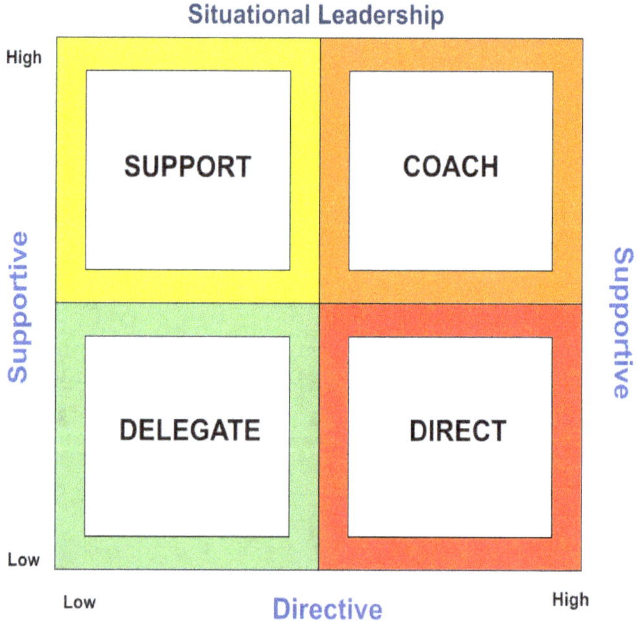

By understanding **Situational Leadership®** (Davis, n.d.) principles, I became equipped to synthesize the readiness and capabilities of the people I was leading, learn from them, and adjust my leadership approach accordingly. Whether someone requires more guidance and direction or thrives with greater autonomy, Situational Leadership® empowers me as a leader to tailor my interactions and support to best meet individual needs.

Hey, guess what? Embracing Situational Leadership® turned me into a versatile leader, ready to tackle any multifarious challenge. Each role was a learning adventure, preparing me for the next thing. Not knowing through the ups and downs, I was being prepared for the upcoming opportunity. It's like building blocks, one role at a time. You will be building pieces for your foundation and elevating your talent. To nurture your talent, especially in leadership, is to exceed expectations. Learning from past experiences has not just boosted my skills but also made me a more effective leader, ready to inspire in any situation. So, dive into the journey, soak up those experiences, and watch yourself soar as a leader! To my young adult readers in high school or college, if you desire to cultivate leading others, using Situational Leadership®, take the time to pull the research to identify the quadrants and how this can be incorporated into your school, athletic, or organization leadership role.

Developing TalentFRED was the culmination of synthesizing all the lessons and experiences from my previous roles. It enabled me to recognize my inherent value and the impact I can make, serving as the core of my

ikigai and personal development journey. So, my advice to you in nurturing your leadership talent will be to gain an array of tools and strategies necessary for your talent toolbelt as a leader.

In conclusion, I want you to explore mastering self-leadership as an initial step toward effectively leading others. Once you've established your own cadence and best practices, it's vital to share your strategies for success by mentoring or coaching anyone ready to receive and grow their talent in leadership.

Now that we've covered some ground in previous chapters, as a leader, utilize your leadership style to lift others and grow their talent. Don't be selfish in your strategies—it's about empowering those around you, helping them grow, and building a legacy of leadership excellence.

If you do it right, your superpower can become the result of your leadership style. How can you use it to bring out the best in people? How can you inspire growth and development? Picture it as a ripple effect—the impact you make now echoes into the future. I know you are ready to go into exploration mode to contribute something bigger and make it transcend you. It's not just leadership; it's about creating a legacy of excellence. Are you ready to make your mark? Let's GO!

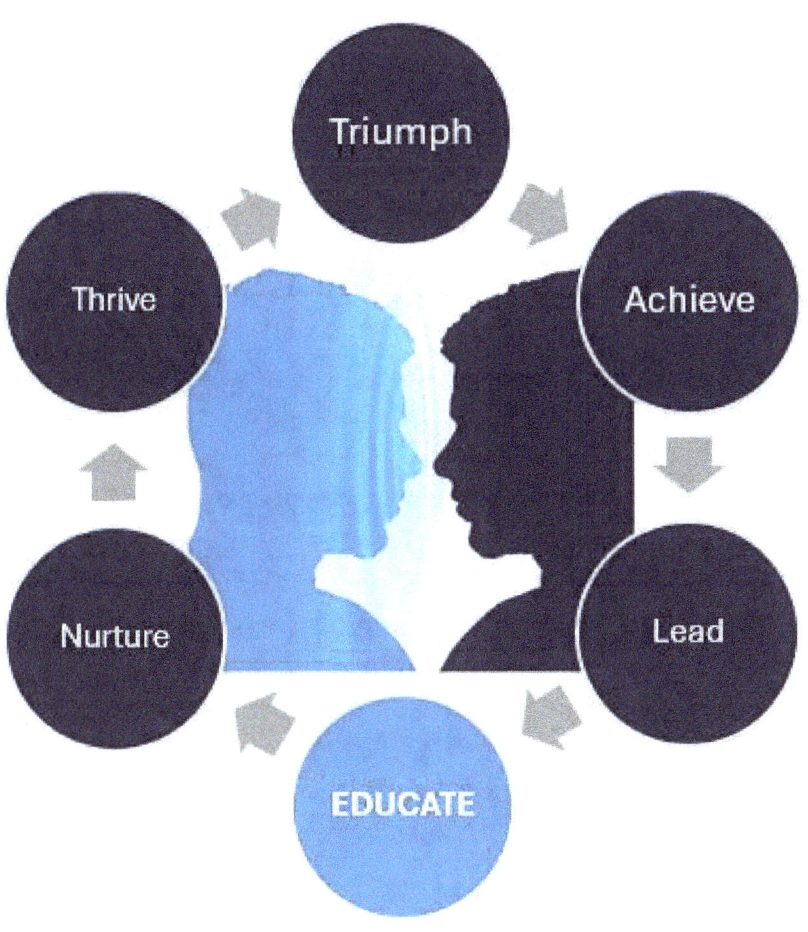
Triumph
Thrive
Achieve
Nurture
Lead
EDUCATE

In this chapter, we will investigate the importance of education and continuous learning in the pursuit of nurturing and developing your talent. In today's rapidly evolving world, where industries are constantly changing and new technologies emerge at a staggering pace, the ability to adapt and grow is paramount. As you aspire to become an effective individual in your job, career, professional journey, or personal growth benchmarks, the journey begins with a commitment to *educating you*.

As a lifelong educator, I've dedicated myself to continuous learning and professional development, this is a core of TalentFRED. Through classes, workshops, conferences, and obtaining degrees and certifications, I've enriched my skills and talents. This commitment has not only enhanced my teaching practice but also inspired my students to embrace lifelong learning. I was also able to transcend many opportunities in my career and fraternal life. It's a testament to the transformative power of education and the impact dedicated people can have on future generations.

Sharpening Your Goals:

Setting clear and achievable goals are critical for growing your talent. Whether you're embarking on a new career path, pursuing further education, or striving to enhance your skills, sharpening your goals provides direction and motivation.

Here are some steps to help you refine your goal:

Your Steps	Talent Actions
Reflect on Your Passions and Values	<ul><li>Take time to identify what truly inspires and motivates you.</li><li>Consider your interests, values, and long-term aspirations.</li><li>Align your goals with these core aspects of yourself to ensure they resonate deeply.</li></ul>
Make Your Goals Specific and Measurable	<ul><li>Clearly define what you want to achieve and establish measurable criteria for success.</li><li>Instead of setting vague goals like "improve my skills," specify exactly what skills you want to develop and how you will measure progress.</li></ul>
Break Down Your Goals into Smaller Tasks	<ul><li>Break larger goals into manageable tasks or milestones.</li><li>This makes them less daunting and allows you to track progress more effectively.</li><li>Create a timeline for completing each task and hold yourself accountable.</li></ul>
Prioritize Your Goals	<ul><li>Not all goals are equal in importance or urgency.</li><li>Prioritize your goals based on their significance and relevance to your overall objectives.</li><li>Focus on those that will have the</li></ul>

	greatest impact on your personal and professional development.
Stay Flexible and Adapt to Change	<ul><li>While it's important to set goals, it's equally crucial to remain adaptable in the face of unforeseen circumstances or new opportunities.</li><li>Be willing to adjust your goals as needed and embrace changes that may lead to better outcomes.</li></ul>
Seek Support and Accountability	<ul><li>Share your goals with trusted friends, mentors, or colleagues who can offer encouragement and support.</li><li>Consider joining a community or finding an accountability partner to help you stay motivated and accountable.</li></ul>
Celebrate Your Achievements	<ul><li>Acknowledge and celebrate your progress along the way.</li><li>Each milestone reached is a testament to your dedication and hard work.</li><li>Take time to recognize your accomplishments and use them as fuel to propel you toward your next goal.</li></ul>

Exploring Resources:

Aren't we lucky in today's world? To cultivate your *talent*, you have too many learning opportunities, which are convenient with online courses, books, podcasts, and workshops. My suggestion *is that it is not what you use for learning, as long as you use resources that suit your style.* And here's a tip: don't go solo; find mentors and communities to guide and cheer you on. I've discovered some awesome resources in my career journey; it's like having a talent-boosting toolkit.

Today, educating yourself is enriching, thanks to the internet. Learning materials and platforms are abundant, covering diverse interests and skill levels—all from the comfort of your home.

Online Courses	*LinkedIn Learning*
Videos	*Podcasts*
Books	*Seminars/Workshops*
Conferences	*Networking*

Developing a Learning Routine:

Let's chat about a game-changer: ensuring consistency in your learning journey. Trust me, building atomic habits pays off big time. Picture this: setting aside regular time to plunge into learning activities.

Think of it like a date with knowledge—commit and show up! Treat your education like you would a formal academic pursuit, with that same dedication and respect. Personally, this has been a strong attribute for me, but I understand for some this will be a challenge. When I didn't build strong habits and a solid routine, mastering skills in visual arts, music, teaching, math, technology, you name it, became a real challenge. *So, make a pact to be consistent and watch those goals turn into wins*!

Activity 4A: Routine Flowchart

(By following these steps and consistently dedicating time to your learning routine, you'll be able to make steady progress towards your goals and develop new skills and knowledge effectively.)

Which goal are you working on?		
When are you going to work the routine?	__ M __ T __ W __ R __ F __ Sat	☐ Morning ☐ Afternoon ☐ Evening
What resources will be needed?		
What tasks or techniques are you practicing?		
What is your reflection on the goal and activities?		

Embracing Challenges:

Mastering desired skills and your overall talent is no walk in the park. Expect bumps in the road—obstacles and setbacks that challenge your **ikigai**. Embrace these hiccups as chances to grow and learn. Don't shy away from pushing your boundaries or tackling robust concepts or skills. Keep in mind that every mistake is a lesson that inches you closer to mastering your talent.

★ *FRED: I faced challenges during my first few months as a Solution Engineer for an EdTech company, especially with the need to learn multiple software programs and scripts quickly while also mastering the art of presenting to customers effectively. Here's how I leveraged my experiences and observations to establish a more focused and productive routine: I accepted each challenge, established a routine, adapted to customers, sought feedback, and improved continuously.*

Measuring Progress:

When measuring progress, some may be concerned about the how-tos; is this too academic? You can't keep up and may view it as just another issue to deal with in your daily life. Well, my suggestion to you in growing your gift is to check your development on a frequent basis. We discussed earlier that you have to set clear goals that match what you want to learn and keep track of how you're doing. You can't skip this essential phase. As you are measuring all your small successes, celebrate your wins—they're like milestones in your learning journey. You have to face it and understand that setbacks happen but use them to fuel you and motivate you to try even harder. Stay accountable, stay focused, and keep learning with enthusiasm. You'll make big strides toward reaching your full potential.

As a teacher, I monitored my students' progress and reflected on my strategies that effectively brought concepts and content to life in the classroom. Utilizing various tools, charts, and other resources became integral to accurately tracking their progress and understanding why certain answers or concepts were achieved higher or lower than the benchmarks. I quickly learned that I was inspired by this routine. To grow TalentFRED, I extended the same process to my growth and development, actively involving teachers, coaches and mentors to enhance my skills in instruction, professional development, leadership, student and adult learning, as well as technology integration. My advice to you in regard to measuring progress is the following, adopting an efficient approach ensures continuous improvement. As Stephen Covey said, begin with the end in mind. And TalentFRED, learn what happened in your process to get to that end goal.

Measuring your progress in talent and personal development demands a combination of tenacity, consistency, and genuine self-reflection.

As you develop the steps of Educating YOU, this step stands out as a formidable talent instrument, granting you the autonomy to formulate and lead your journey. Aligning your educational efforts with your specific objectives is what I call "*aligning to your design.*" Not only will you gain a deeper understanding of your talent, but you will also foster a sense of ownership and command over your development. Exploring a myriad of resources allow you to tailor your learning experience to your unique preferences and areas of interest.

Educating you to formulate your talent(s) means developing an organized learning routine that is crucial to maintaining momentum and discipline. It will empower you to have consistency, which supports the retention of knowledge. To develop your talent, you will need to have robust and positive habits and a conducive environment for ongoing growth. To enrich educating you, I want you to keep this in mind: mastering anything requires sticking with it and staying dedicated. Every challenge you face is a chance to learn and get better. *The best armor for mastery is persistence.* Embrace the challenges—they're steppingstones to refining your talent.

Just so you know, the E in my name, is all about education, and the D in my name stands for developing appreciation. It's my way of expressing a commitment to both learning and fostering a deeper understanding or admiration for building my talent. I just thought I'd clue you in on my personalized analogy and insight!

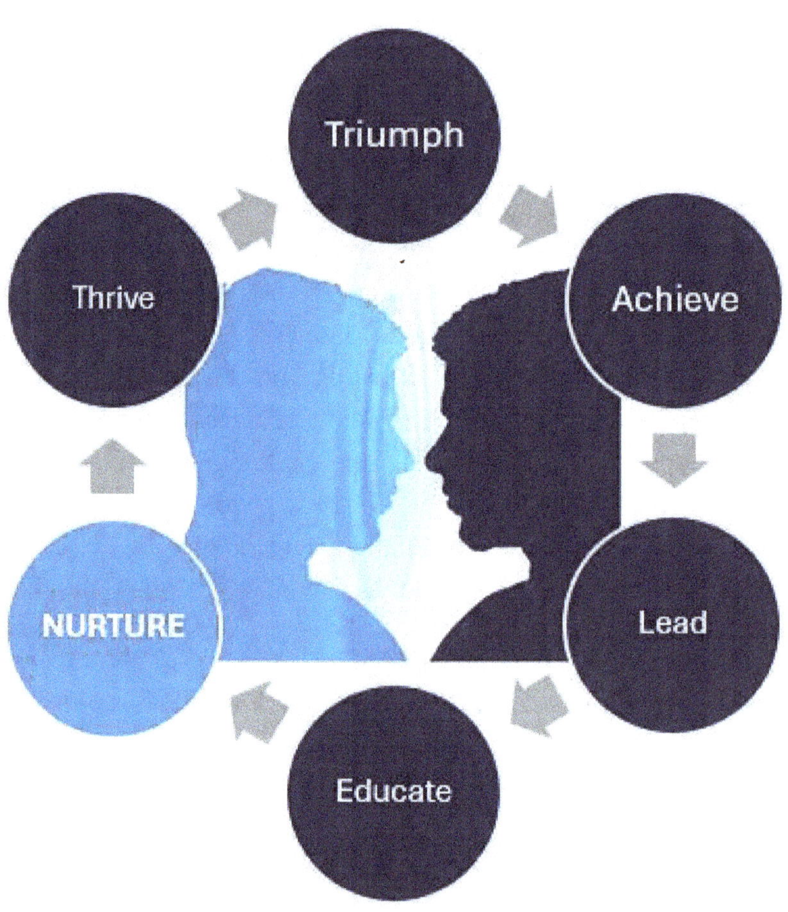

Triumph
Thrive
Achieve
NURTURE
Lead
Educate

In this chapter, we will synthesize the pivotal role you can play in knowing who you are socially, emotionally, and physically. This is an element that enhances or decreases the opportunity to grow your talent. **Nurturing yourself** is not just beneficial; it's essential for your overall well-being and development. If you are not taking care of yourself, your talent can stall or, even worse, stop on its track.

In my life's journey of nurturing me, I came to realize the importance of balancing my vigorous drive for achievement with caring for my mental and physical well-

being. Indeed, it's common for anyone, especially in their younger years, to prioritize their aspirations and constantly chase after new opportunities without considering the long-term toll it may take on their overall health.

The human body is a complex and phenomenal machine, but it requires care and maintenance to function optimally. Ignoring the signs of fatigue or neglecting social, emotional, or physical practices can eventually lead to burnout. This is why this chapter is critical to your talent. All the efforts from the previous stages can be in jeopardy if you are not nurturing yourself.

Exercise 5A: Care Plan for Yourself

Date Started: _______
Celebration Completion Date: _____________

Area of Focus	What would energize you?	How often and when would I perform the activity?	What resource(s) are needed?	How will you measure your success?
Social Target				
Emotional Target				
Physical Target				
Additional Target				
Additional Target				
***Select:** Daily, Weekly, Monthly or Combination*				

Creating, implementing, and monitoring a self-care plan is like giving yourself a VIP pass to feel great. Whether it's enjoying a cup of coffee, wine, taking a quick nap, small acts of self-love add up to big-time bliss. So, treat yourself well, because self-care is the ultimate game-changer.

My immediate advice is to find a balance. Incorporating habits that boost your mental and physical well-being, such as regular exercise, adequate rest, mindfulness practices, and setting boundaries around work and personal time, can help prevent burnout and sustain your energy levels in the long run.

It does not matter your age or gender in life, please prioritize yourself and listen to the needs of your body and mind, you'll not only enhance your overall health and happiness but also ensure that you're able to continue pursuing your targets to cultivate your **own talent**.

A serious life lesson brought me to a halt. I remember in August 2021, I was not feeling 100% and becoming thirsty, as well as craving sodas, sweets, chips, and more. It was not normal for me to crave these items 24/7. Being in a new role at work as a Solution Engineer for PowerSchool as well as the State President of my fraternity (*Alpha Phi Alpha Fraternity, Inc. - Virginia*), I never slowed down or stopped to reflect on or investigate what was going on with my physical health. One of my fraternity brothers, who is a doctor, just so happened to call me to check on how I was doing, I disclosed to him my desire to drink all day, especially soft drinks, and eat all day long into the night. He suggested that I contact my primary doctor immediately to assess what was happening. At the doctor's office, blood was drawn to assess my glucose level, etc. My doctor came into the room looking concerned yet firm. I was not as coherent that day and extremely sleepy. To focus on his words and hear him logically was a challenge I had not experienced before. The news he presented was jaw-dropping. My blood sugar levels were extremely high, above 375, and my A1c was 12.9. Additionally, my blood pressure and weight were the highest they had ever been in my life. Not completely knowing what the numbers meant, I knew the medical information he was sharing was not good. My memory of my father having the same issue at around the same age resonated with me immediately, and I needed to change. When the doctor shared that he was afraid that another day on this course, I could have possibly died, I knew right then that I needed to **nurture myself** and quickly make some systematic changes for myself.

Sitting there and listening to my physician was humbling yet eye-opening. I needed to do everything necessary to get back to my health. This included taking new medications to control my blood sugar and cholesterol. There would be no way I could accomplish any professional or fraternal goals unless I nurtured myself. My loving wife stepped in to assist me on my journey as a *call to action*.

I'm thrilled about my personal achievements and the discipline it took to accomplish my health goals. A key strategy I used to support my health was engaging with an endocrinologist and seeking guidance from online health coaches on YouTube. To nurture my talents and achieve personal growth, I focused on strategies to elevate my life.

Nurturing yourself involves a holistic approach that addresses your physical, mental, emotional, and spiritual needs.

Here are some ways you can nurture yourself:

- ★ **Take Care of Yourself:**
  - ○ Try activities like meditation, exercise, healthy eating, and good sleep.
  - ○ Recharge your energy, reduce stress, and boost overall well-being.
- ★ **Set Healthy Boundaries for Yourself:**
  - ○ Learn to say no to draining commitments.
  - ○ Guard your time and mental space to focus on what brings you joy.
- ★ **Stay Mindful and Self-Aware of Yourself:**
  - ○ Just focus on what's happening right now.
  - ○ Pay attention to your thoughts and emotions without judgment.
- ★ **Seek Support of You:**
  - ○ Surround yourself with uplifting friends, family, or mentors.
  - ○ Share your journey for valuable perspectives and emotional support.
- ★ **Keep Learning and Growing You:**
  - ○ Invest in personal and professional interests.
  - ○ Lifelong learning keeps your mind engaged and having purpose.

★ **Be Kind to Yourself:**
- ○ Practice self-compassion.
- ○ Treat yourself as kindly as you would a friend facing similar situations.

★ **Connect Yourself with Nature:**
- ○ Spend time outdoors according to your comfort zone for a calming and rejuvenating effect.

★ **Express Your Creativity:**
- ○ Engage in a hobby you enjoy. Let your creativity flow freely, expressing your thoughts and finding joy in the process.

Remember that nurturing yourself is not selfish; if you do not nurture yourself, no one else will. A philosophy I adopted has been to learn to listen and listen to learn what your body is telling you. Prioritize your social, emotional, and physical well-being and make it a non-negotiable part of your life.

There is a song by Incognito called "*True to Yourself*" that says, "*If I gotta be true to no other I gotta be true to myself.*" Being true to yourself is paramount, and part of that is nurturing and caring for yourself. It's about honoring your needs, values, and aspirations, and prioritizing your well-being on your journey toward personal growth and fulfillment. Keep staying true to yourself and nurturing your innermost being—it's the foundation for a truly fulfilling life.

Triumph
Achieve
THRIVE
Lead
Nurture
Educate

Inspired by Maya Angelou's words, '*My mission in life is not merely to survive, but to thrive; and to do so with some passion, some compassion, some humor, and some style,*' I've come to realize the significance of knowing and appreciating my talent in my life's journey. It's key for you to seize every opportunity for growth, education, and reflection. This steadfast approach not only allowed me to achieve my best, but also added depth and richness to my life, characterized by passion, compassion, humor, and style. At this stage, you want to think about how you can thrive beyond your expectations. Don't listen to or consider the opinions of others regarding your passions, desires, or more. Your talent is unique to you. Thriving and being persistent in executing your talent will make you feel like you won the lottery!!!

Here is my personal reflection and life experience:

Throughout my life, I've always been driven by a desire to surpass my capabilities and defy expectations. Whenever someone said, "You can't," I'd silently respond, "I can, and I'll do it even better than you think." This inner fire has fueled me in every aspect of my life—academically, personally, and professionally.

One pivotal moment stands out: when my high school counselor told me I wasn't good enough for college. Instead of letting that discourage me, it ignited a determination to prove them wrong. Choosing to attend Hampton University, an HBCU, not only exposed me to a community of high-achieving African Americans but also reinforced my belief that surrounding myself with excellence would help me achieve it myself.

My college experience wasn't just about earning a degree; it was about defying expectations and demonstrating that I could thrive despite the doubts cast upon me. And more than that, it was about using my journey to inspire others to do the same—to push past limitations and strive for greatness.

So, I continue to push boundaries, exceed expectations, and motivate others along the way to reach their TalentFRED. My story isn't just about personal success; it's about empowering others to believe in themselves and their potential. And that's a journey worth sharing and celebrating.

Thriving means constantly growing, developing, and staying resilient, as well as inspiring others to do the same. So how do we take your talent beyond you? Taking it beyond you involves creating a ripple effect of growth and resilience that extends to others. It's about sharing your story, and knowledge, providing support, and empowering others to embrace their own journeys and talent development. I believe we should foster a culture of encouragement and collaboration, so we can collectively elevate each other to higher levels of success and fulfillment. Again, assisting each other to know their ikigai.

Have you ever heard of
**Maslow's Hierarchy of Needs
(Vernon, n.d.)**? It is a ladder for
our wants and needs. At the
bottom are the must-haves.
Move up the ladder, and there's a
need for security. Keep
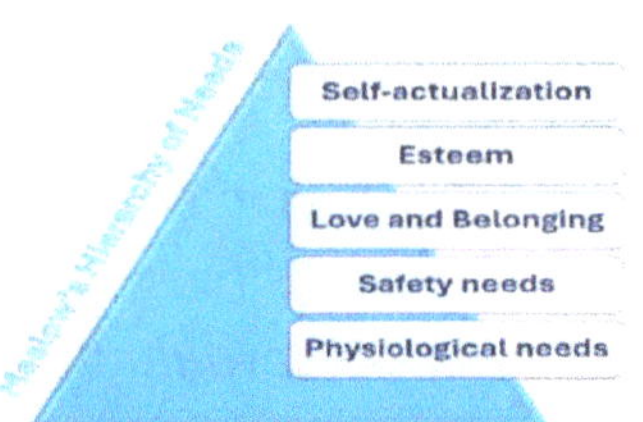

climbing, and you'll hit the desire for love and connection.
Then, it's about feeling good about yourself and getting
respect. The very top? That's all about personal growth and
feeling fulfilled. It's a roadmap that says we try to get these
things in a specific order, one step at a time.

*Take this advice: if you continue to improve your
skills on a regular basis, you will not just become proficient
at what you do.*

You are reaching higher-level needs, like feeling
respected and achieving self-actualization. When you
consistently show off your talent, you get the respect and
recognition you crave—fulfilling that esteem need. There
will be nothing better than hearing from others
acknowledging your talent. There are many performing
artists who say that they feel exuberant when an audience
applauds their performance. We all want to be applauded.
Additionally, as you keep growing, going up the ladder of
crafting your talents, you're reaching the top of Maslow's
Hierarchy of Needs—self-actualization. So, investing in
your talents isn't just personal growth; it's like creating a
roadmap to thrive and reach new levels of success and
fulfillment.

What does it take to thrive beyond you? Thriving beyond your standards requires these **four key elements:**

Now, I want to complete this Activity 6A:

Vision and Purpose	Continuous Learning
Have a clear vision of what you want to achieve and a strong sense of purpose that drives your actions. Understanding why you do what you do can provide the motivation needed to go beyond the ordinary.	Commit to lifelong learning and personal development. Stay curious, seek new knowledge, and be open to different perspectives. This will help you adapt to changes and stay ahead in your field.
One Word for Your Purpose:	*One Word for Your Learning:*
Resilience	**Passion and Persistence**
Develop resilience to overcome setbacks and obstacles. Understand that failure is a part of the journey towards success. Learn from your mistakes, bounce back stronger, and keep moving forward with determination.	Pursue your goals with passion and dedication. Stay committed to your vision, even when faced with challenges or setbacks. Persistence is often the key to overcoming obstacles and achieving long-term success.
One Word for Motivate Your Resilience:	*One Word for Motivate Your Passion/Persistence:*

Remember this: no one can be you. Embracing your uniqueness and striving to surpass your limitations will empower you, bring joy, and fuel your motivation to achieve the seemingly impossible. As you nurture your talents and abilities, you'll unlock new possibilities and reach heights you once thought unattainable. So, embrace your individuality, thrive beyond your limits, and watch as your potential unfolds in remarkable ways.

Thriving also means exploring diverse skills and career opportunities. It boosts adaptability, resilience, and growth. My advice to you is to embrace the journey, seize opportunities, and find fulfillment in the diversity of experiences.

Diversifying your skills and career pathway means broadening your expertise and exploring different professional avenues, which enhances adaptability and flexibility in the job market. Ensure you gain the necessary skills and foundation for each talent opportunity.

In my journey to cultivate my talent, I've focused on nurturing my desires, developing desired skills, building strong abilities, boosting self-esteem, and teaching others to do the same, as outlined in this book. Document your journey along the way. You will respect the steps and appreciate those times that challenged you. Don't be afraid to go beyond expectations to develop your talent. It will be uncomfortable at times. Many people have heard me say, *"Get comfortable with the uncomfortable."* This statement is my advice to you. Go beyond you by teaching others, mentoring, coaching, and offering professional growth sessions. Thanks to all my coaches in education, technology, and fraternity that assisted me in thriving beyond me for the betterment of myself and especially others.

Reflecting on my experience leading my state fraternity as president, I integrated my talents and skills to employ shared and situational leadership, strategic planning, and coaching others. This inspired many to reach their potential and supported the growth of our membership. Serving as a servant leader in this role empowered me to go beyond myself and continue striving for excellence in the organization.

To thrive beyond your current abilities, consider these practices to enrich your talents:

1. **Embrace Challenges:** Step out of your comfort zone and tackle new challenges. Embracing discomfort fosters growth and resilience, ultimately enhancing your abilities.

   What are some examples for you?
   a. **Public Speaking:** Overcoming the fear of public speaking by regularly volunteering to present in front of groups, which enhances communication skills and confidence.
   b. **Traveling Alone:** Exploring new destinations solo, navigating unfamiliar cultures and languages, fostering independence and adaptability.
   c. **Learning a Musical Instrument:** Dedication to mastering a musical instrument, embracing the challenges of practice and perseverance to achieve proficiency.

d. **Completing a Course:** Taking on a challenging academic course or certification program, pushing through difficulties to expand knowledge and skills.

2.

    What are some examples for you?
    a. **Interning in Various Industries:** Gain exposure to different sectors by interning in industries like marketing, finance, and technology.
    b. **Volunteering in Different Organizations:** Broaden your understanding of social issues and work cultures by volunteering with a variety of organizations, such as non-profits, community centers, and environmental groups.
    c. **Participating in Cross-Functional Projects:** Collaborate on cross-functional projects/activities within your job or academic setting to work with colleagues from different departments, enhance teamwork skills, and foster creativity.

3.

What are some examples for you?

    a. **Volunteer Tutoring:** Offer your expertise in subjects like math, science, or language arts to students in need of academic support. This could involve volunteering at local schools, community centers, or online tutoring platforms.

    b. **Professional Mentoring:** Guide junior colleagues or aspiring professionals in your field by offering advice, sharing insights, and providing career guidance. This could involve formal mentorship programs within your organization or informal mentorship arrangements.

    c. **Workshop Facilitation:** Lead workshops or training sessions to share your expertise on specific topics or skills. This could include topics like public speaking, project management, or software development, depending on your area of expertise.

    d. **Youth Mentorship Programs:** Participate in youth mentorship programs aimed at providing guidance and support to young people in various aspects of their lives, such as education, career planning, or personal development. This has been one of the most rewarding aspects and engagement with others that has inspired my growth.

4. **Networking:** Build and maintain a strong professional network to exchange ideas, collaborate on projects, and discover new opportunities for growth and development.

What are some examples for you?

   a. **Attending Industry Conferences:** Participate in conferences, trade shows, or seminars related to your field. Engage with professionals, exchange contacts, and follow up with connections afterward to foster relationships and explore potential collaborations.

   b. **Joining Professional Associations:** Become a member of industry-specific professional associations or networking groups. Attend networking events, participate in online forums, and take advantage of mentorship programs offered by these organizations to expand your network and stay updated on industry trends.

   c. **Utilizing Social Media Platforms:** Actively engage with professionals in your field on social media platforms like LinkedIn, Facebook, X, or industry-specific forums. Share relevant content, participate in discussions, and connect with individuals with similar interests or expertise to build meaningful relationships.

d. **Informational Interviews:** Reach out to professionals in your desired industry or role to request informational interviews. Use these meetings to learn more about their career paths, seek advice, and expand your network. Additionally, offer to share your own expertise or insights to establish a mutually beneficial relationship.

In conclusion, thriving beyond yourself involves refining your talents to illuminate your ikigai to the world, while also showcasing your value and impact to others.

CONCLUSION

As we conclude our journey in **'TalentFRED: Unveiling Your Potential,'** I hope you've uncovered the hidden gems of talents and potential within you. Throughout this book, we've delved into the importance of introspection, overcoming challenges, exploring diverse experiences, and the impact of sharing knowledge with others to unlock your talent and find your ikigai.

Remember, unveiling your potential isn't just about personal success—it's about using your talents to make a positive impact on the world around you. As you continue your journey, I encourage you to embrace new opportunities, be open to your surroundings as well as those opportunities on your blind side and share your unique gifts with others to elevate their talent.

Whether you're a budding entrepreneur, a seasoned professional, a student, or someone simply seeking to unlock their full potential, know that your journey towards self-discovery and personal growth is ongoing. Keep pushing your boundaries, keep striving for excellence, and above all, keep believing in the power of your talent to shape a brighter future for yourself. I know this world needs your voice and talent.

As a music enthusiast, I've found inspiration in songs that resonate with every aspect of my journey. From self-discovery to embracing challenges and diversifying experiences, tunes like *"You Never Stand Alone" by Whitney Houston, "Optimistic" by Sounds of Blackness, "Simply The Best" by Tina Turner, "Keep On Movin" by Soul II Soul, "Sometimes" by Anita Baker, or "Don't Stop Believin" by Journey* have uplifted and motivated me. Songs like these can amplify your drive as you navigate the suggested guidelines, providing the soundtrack to your journey toward realizing your full potential.

I was blessed to have dynamic parents who gave me phenomenal life messages. Here are two poignant statements from my mom and dad:

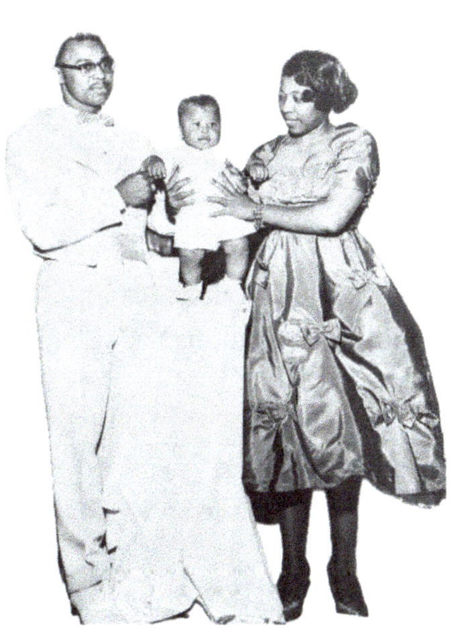

· My mother, **Rochelle W. Scott**, said, "*I want you to do your best and then say, don't play me cheap.*" People will place you in a box or try to determine your worth or value. Prove them wrong by achieving the unexpected.

· My father, **Fred W. Scott, Sr.**, told me to pursue my dreams and aspirations, but don't wake up one morning saying, "*I wish I woulda, coulda. This is your life, and no dress rehearsal.*"

Thank you for joining me on this transformative journey. Be optimistic, go forth, and unleash your Talent and Unveil Your Potential!

- ❖ **Triumphing You (T):** Empower yourself to overcome challenges and obstacles and emerge victorious in your personal and professional endeavors.
- ❖ **Achieving Your Best (A):** Implement strategies and tools to help you set and achieve meaningful goals, unlocking your full potential.
- ❖ **Leading You & Others (L):** Apply leadership skills to lead yourself effectively while inspiring others toward success.
- ❖ **Educating You (E):** Facilitate continuous learning and growth, enabling you to expand your knowledge and skills to thrive in your chosen fields.
- ❖ **Nurturing You (N):** Foster self-care, wellness, and resilience to maintain a healthy work-life balance and overall well-being.
- ❖ **Thriving Beyond You (T):** Encourage yourself to build a stronger you to rise above expectations and contribute to a brighter future.

Use this affirmation…

I will triumph, I will achieve, I will lead, educate, nurture myself, and thrive beyond my expectations.

<u>Bibliography/References/Copyright</u>

- *About – Founder-3T – Medium*. (n.d.). Medium. https://medium.com/@3T_Collective/about
- Adminiolita. (2022, May 27). *Self-Development Ikigai: the meaning of life*. Zekluu. https://zekluu.com/en/self-development-ikigai-el-sentido-de-la-vida/
- Akṣapāda. (2019). *Maya Angelou's Celebration of Words: 1001 Expressions of an Uncaged Bird*.
- *All about your A1C*. (2018, August 21). Centers for Disease Control and Prevention. https://www.cdc.gov/diabetes/managing/managing-blood-sugar/a1c.html
- Boogaard, K. (2024, February 6). *How to write SMART goals (with examples)*. Work Life by Atlassian. https://www.atlassian.com/blog/productivity/how-to-write-smart-goals#:~:text=What%20are%20SMART%20goals%3F,within%20a%20certain%20time%20frame.
- Clear, J. (2018). *Atomic habits: the life-changing million-copy #1 bestseller*. Random House.

- *Create your personal strategic plan.* (n.d.). ASAE. https://www.asaecenter.org/association-careerhq/career/articles/career-management/create-your-personal-strategic-plan
- *Habit Formation: Building Better Habits: The Daily Factor Approach - FasterCapital.* (n.d.). FasterCapital. https://fastercapital.com/content/Habit-Formation--Building-Better-Habits--The-Daily-Factor-Approach.html
- *Habitica - Gamify your life.* (n.d.). https://habitica.com/
- *Habitify: Personalized Habit Tracker App | Build Better Habits Today.* (n.d.). https://www.habitify.me/
- LeBrun, J. (2017, June 11). The behavioral science behind Pillsy - Jeff LeBrun - medium. *Medium.* https://medium.com/@jeffleb/the-behavioral-science-behind-pillsy-d9ce4c47993d
- Maslow, A. (1974). *A theory of human motivation.* Lulu.com.
- *MindTools | Home.* (n.d.-a). https://www.mindtools.com/a4wo118/smart-goals
- *MindTools | Home.* (n.d.-b). https://www.mindtools.com/amtbj63/swot-analysis
- Minutes. (2015). *Maslow's hierarchy of needs: Gain vital insights into how to motivate people.* 50 Minutes.
- MSEd, K. C. (2023, June 27). *How to Lead: 6 Leadership Styles and Frameworks.* Verywell

Mind. https://www.verywellmind.com/leadership-styles-2795312

- Resource Complete. (2021, October 12). *What is Self Leadership?* Resource Complete | Human Capital Resource Solutions. https://resourcecomplete.com/what-is-self-leadership/
- Simply Psychology. (2024, January 24). *Maslow's Hierarchy of Needs.* https://www.simplypsychology.org/maslow.html
- Steward, H. L., Bethea, M., MD, Andrews, S., MD, & Balart, L., MD. (2003). *The new Sugar Busters!: Cut Sugar to Trim Fat.* Ballantine Books.
- *STREAKS. The to-do list that helps you form good habits. For iOS.* (n.d.). Streaks. https://streaksapp.com/
- The Center for Leadership Studies. (2024, February 16). *Situational Leadership® | What is Situational Leadership®.* Situational Leadership® Management and Leadership Training. https://situational.com/situational-leadership/
- Wen, J., & Wen, J. (2024, February 6). The 6 most common leadership styles & How to find yours. *IMD business school for management and leadership courses.* https://www.imd.org/reflections/leadership-styles/
- Wikipedia contributors. (2024, February 24). *Ikigai.* Wikipedia. https://en.wikipedia.org/wiki/Ikigai

MY TAKEAWAYS

| Chapter 1 | Triumphing YOU |

- ____
____
____

| Chapter 2 | Achieving YOU |

- ____
____
____

| Chapter 3 | Leading YOU & Others |

- ____
____
____

| Chapter 4 | Educating YOU |

- ____
____
____

| Chapter 5 | Nurturing YOU |

- ____
____
____

| Chapter 6 | Thriving Beyong YOU |

- ____
____
____

TALENT "BRAIN DUMP" IDEAS

HOME

- _______________________________________
- _______________________________________
- _______________________________________

PERSONAL

- _______________________________________
- _______________________________________
- _______________________________________

PROFESSIONAL

- _______________________________________
- _______________________________________
- _______________________________________

FINANCIAL

- _______________________________________
- _______________________________________
- _______________________________________

HEALTH

- _______________________________________
- _______________________________________
- _______________________________________

SCHOOL

- _______________________________________
- _______________________________________
- _______________________________________

OTHER

- _______________________________________
- _______________________________________
- _______________________________________

MY PERSONAL TIMELINE

Time/Day/Month	Main Tasks/Goals	My Measure of Success

MY LETTER TO YOU

Dear READER,

I am so proud of you for spending the time and effort to explore my book. I appreciate you reading and applying the strategies to your career, personal growth, school, or profession. The key to unlocking your potential is to create value and impact in everything you do to become the best version of yourself. Your commitment to growth and embracing new opportunities for self-investment is valuable.

You are the best person to lead your own life. Remember, *life is not a dress rehearsal.* Celebrate all successes and learn from those opportunities where you fail. Your "**ikigai**" will make an impact in this world. My book aims to guide you in developing or enhancing your skills and talents. I empower you to mentor others to enrich their mindsets and skill sets.

I recommend surrounding yourself with authentic mentors, coaches, colleagues, and friends who can provide honest feedback and support your goals and strengths.

You will **triumph, achieve, lead, educate, nurture, and thrive** beyond your expectations.

God bless you with your endeavors to unveil your talent.

Love,

Fred Scott

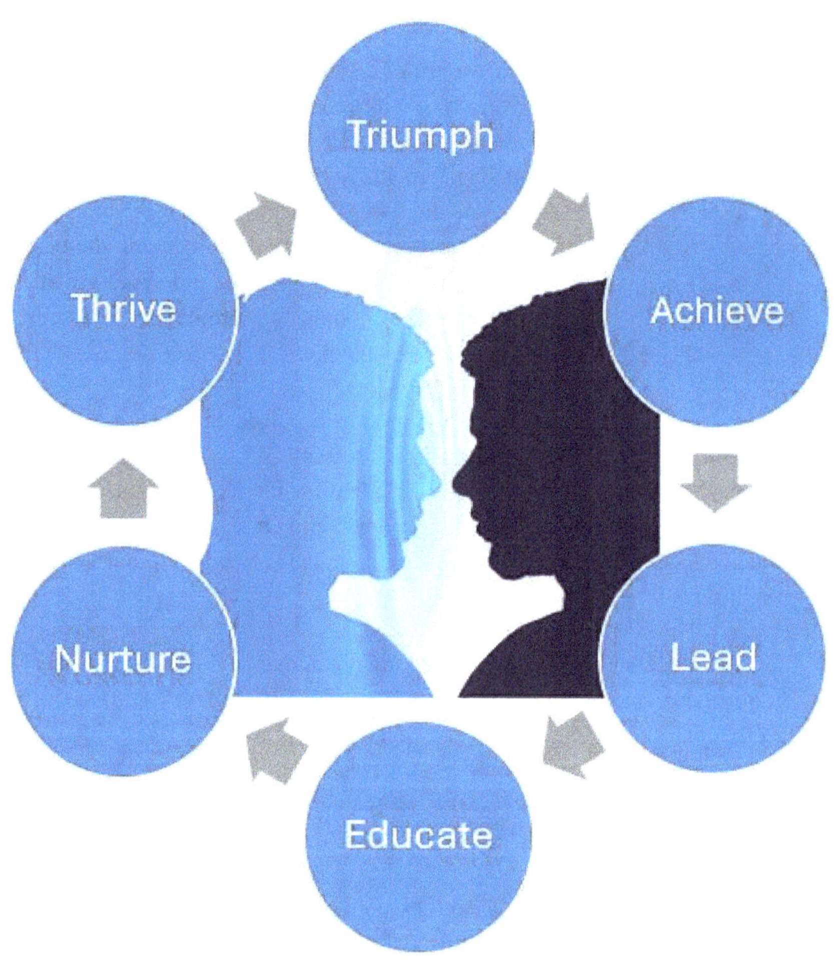
Triumph
Thrive
Achieve
Nurture
Lead
Educate